I0412844

INTELLECTUAL STERILIZATION

DARYL E. RICE

CONTENTS

PREFACE

My objective in writing this book is to address the issue of intellect as it pertains to African-Americans. It is based on the many years of studying and researching the discipline of African-American Studies. As an African-American I have a vested interest in the overall level of the intellect of my people. I am cognizant of the many highly intellectual African-Americans of the past as well as of today. As a matter of fact, they serve as an influence to me in writing this book.

My journey in writing this book was birthed through studying intellect, linguistics, anthropology, ancient Egypt, and the history of my people on this planet. I began to question how we as a people went from being the progenitors of civilization to so many of my brothers filling prison cells across this country. As a child raised by my mother, without ever knowing my father, I often wondered why so many fathers were and still are missing in my community. Through twenty-plus years of study and research, I began to conclude that something has happened to our intellect. It is as if a sterilization of the intellect has been launched on us—in many cases without us being aware of it. A powerless mind is the result of the sterilization process. This book features information that will give credence to this idea of the sterilization of the African-American intellect as well solutions that will invoke change. If you have ever desired to become an intellectually smarter person, this book is written just for you.

ACKNOWLEDGEMENTS

First I would like to thank my mother, Victoria McMillian, for giving birth to me and for always pushing education on me and as well as on my siblings. My mother is no longer with us, and I miss her dearly. It is to her that I dedicate this book. I will always love and never forget my mother.

I thank my lovely wife, Barbara (Lisa) and my wonderful children, Amia and Jaylen, for your continued love and support. You all make my life worth living, and I profess my love for you daily.

To my siblings, Victor, Sandra, Terry, Gail, Charles, and Stennitt, I thank you all for loving me as your brother and for sharing the greatest mother in the world with me. I love you all.

Special thanks go to my best man, Jeff Lewis, for always believing in me and for appreciating my intellect. We are definitely brothers from two different mothers.

To my mentors and friends Bobby Hemmitt and Dr. Walter Williams, thank you for your teachings and guidance. Both of you have helped guide me and educate me on the intellectual power of reading and research. Collectively, both of you have changed my life forever, and my intellect thanks you as well.

Byron Pettit, thank you for taking the time and responsibility of being the first set of eyes to edit my manuscript. Your efforts mean a lot to me. You are a good brother.

Finally, I would like to thank my many family and friends who have always and continue to be in my corner. Your support and relationship will always have a special place within me.

Thank you for your support.
Daryl E. Rice

CHAPTER 1:
EDUCATIONAL STANDARDS

Academics serve as the foundation of measurement in conversations about intelligence. Academic standards establish the platform from which this foundation takes its form. In the general African-American community, academic standards are not a priority in many households. The behavior of many urban youth shows they do not value academics. Many African-American youth are not reading on grade level. Oftentimes, these youth do not strive to change how they are perceived academically. The perception of being an intellectual is not a priority. The perception of being a thug is very prominent today with young African-American males. They appear to lack the discipline to become an intellectual based on their academics.

I attribute this academic downfall in the African-American community to a lack of knowledge of self. In other words, we do not know our history on this planet—not just American history, but also the history of our African heritage. There is a lack of intellectual role models who can cultivate academic prowess and intellectual fortitude. Parents need to create an expectation of high academic achievement in their homes. Intellect is the key component in a person's makeup that can aid in success and overcome all academic roadblocks that may arise in their lives. Academic standards in our households must change and be integrated into the academic lives of our children. Adults should always maintain an academic standard for themselves to cultivate their intellectual capacity. Possessing high academic standards will help build intellect as these standards are attempted to be obtained.

This book is written to institute a change in the way that we think and to raise our intellect to a much higher plateau. As your intellect changes your behavior, your values, self-dignity, and integrity will change as well. This transformation of change can help an individual, a people, and a community.

CHAPTER 2:
ENVIRONMENTAL INFLUENCES AND YOUR INTELLECT

The environmental influences that affect intellectual cultivation in the African-American community cannot be ignored. There are three main issues that need to be addressed in order for my perspective on the community to be validated: crime, racism, and drugs.

Crime has been an issue in the African-American community for several decades. It is an issue for all of America, but Black–on–Black crime is an issue that speaks to the heart of the African-American community.

The breeding process and the breaking down of Africans during slavery remains part of the psyche of African-Americans. The Willie Lynch Syndrome is the second major player in why we continue to harm one another without any sense of love on any level. The Willie Lynch syndrome is a manifestation of the Willie Lynch Letter: The Making of a Slave. This guide to controlling African slaves was written by Mr. Lynch and presented to other slaveholders in the South. The letter gave a "foolproof method" of controlling slaves. It also addressed the importance of creating friction between the old and young slave, light-skin versus dark-skin and removing the male figure from the family unit.

This document is readily available throughout the internet and in book form. I highly recommend that you obtain a copy and read it. The authenticity of this document is debatable, but the question you should ask yourself after reading it is, Is it true? My answer to this question is absolutely. This document is a "must read." The indoctrination of slavery introduced the racism and prejudice factors interracially and intraracially, respectively. Within the race, self-hatred and prejudice define this intra-divisiveness.

Drug usage and distribution is the third key factor because of the effects on the community as a whole. The sale of drugs within our community can be viewed as a promotion of genocide. Usage is also detrimental because of its effects on the user and the family of the user.

Crime, racism, and drugs help impede intellectual growth and development because they all promote nonacademic, nonscholastic and no-loving aspects of the African-American community. It is as if we do not have any cultural integrity of higher intelligence. How do we reverse these issues in our community? How does the greater society view us from an intellectual perspective? How can we make academics and scholarship the main focal points in our community? I will provide answers and solutions to these questions and many others as you continue your journey through this book.

CHAPTER 3:
BOOKS AND THE APPARENT
INTELLECTUAL DECLINE

Literature, in terms of actual books that you read, has an effect on the level of intellect that you have. The great majority of people tend to read fiction books, the Bible, or nothing at all. As African-Americans, we far too often immerse ourselves in the genre of fiction, especially books centered on relationships. This genre does not provide an avenue for intellectual stimulation, but an avenue for emotional stimulation. Emotional stimulation is often substituted for logic. Logic and emotion do not mix from an intellectual standpoint. Fiction books that are extremely popular within the African-American community today cultivate a lack of intellectual knowledge. Fiction is entertainment, not intellectual stimulation. There is absolutely nothing wrong with fulfilling that entertainment need that we all have. The problem arises when this genre of literature is all you read. A lack of knowledge of self continues to be a factor in how we develop intellectually.

The decline of the intellect in the African-American community is staggering. Better academic performance needs to be part of our household standards and expectations. We are not having academic or intellectual conversations with our children at a heightened level. This is the type of conversation that we as parents need to be having with our children on a regular basis. Many of our children believe that being smart or intellectual is not "cool." This mentality cultivates a substandard intellectual and academic mindset. If African-American households would start to have these conversations and encouragements, our children's intellect would begin to flourish.

This goes back to the old cliché "It all starts at home." It is absolutely vital that parents not lose sight of the importance of academics. Parents can create the necessary motivation for their children to achieve higher academic standards. Academic integrity is the foundation for intellectual growth. It is time that we change the way we promote education in our households. It matters not if parents are not college graduates; education should be at the forefront of how we inspire our children to be successful in life.

Increase involvement in your children's educational journey at school. Utilize your local library to give your children a literary avenue to cultivate their reading prowess. Talk to your children daily about what is going on at school. Never forget to ask them, each day, how their day was at school.

Adults can also continue to enhance their intellect by researching the history of Africa and the African Diaspora. You may ask, How does researching and learning about the history of Africa and the African Diaspora contribute to my intellectual growth? Once you learn that you are a descendent of greatness and really allow the vast array of historical facts about this topic to become part of your person, you will articulate and formulate your thoughts differently. Intellect is one of your most powerful aspects in life. Establishing yourself as an intellectual is not just being on top of the academic world; it is being able to use academics and knowledge to change your entire being. You will become a more confident, intellectually diverse, and educationally powerful person than you could ever imagine.

CHAPTER 4:
WHO CONTROLS YOUR THOUGHTS
AND THE INFERIORITY COMPLEX

There are a multitude of images that are absorbed in our minds every day. When cultivating your intelligence, it is important to understand and investigate who controls your thoughts. The school systems throughout America have not educated African-Americans about the greatness of our ancestry. Schools generally promote a Caucasian-centered or Eurocentric worldview. For example, as African-Americans we typically do not see images of us in world leadership positions or positions of significant power. We are not featured in the majority of the literature used by school systems throughout America. By maintaining the European model as the pillar of education, the African-American model of education becomes lost and hidden.

The world around you influences and shapes your thoughts. The danger is when the majority of your thoughts are formulated or enhanced by people who do not look like you, identity problems begin to fester. Your peers can also play a significant role in your thought process. It is always important to associate yourself with individuals that share your goals and morals. Oftentimes listening to your peers can lead to an unfortunate situation for you.

The media is by far the greatest manipulator. It can control your thoughts by presenting a reality that it wants you to believe. Media is not a predominantly African-American owned entity, especially in television media. Black Entertainment Television, for example, is a social pariah; images and portrayals of African-Americans are controlled by non-African-Americans. It is my opinion that the great majority of images of us that are projected from this network are extremely negative. Only recently have I begun to see more positive images and roles being aired on this network

Large numbers of African-Americans have developed an inferiority complex that has proven to be a serious intellectual hurdle. Many African-Americans continue to show signs of wanting to assimilate to the state of being as Caucasian as humanly as possible. For example, African-American women go through a transformation typically about age six of straightening their hair. This need to change the natural state of your hair gives credence to an inferiority complex for African-American women. This also becomes a huge self-esteem issue. Having confidence in oneself provides a solid foundation for intellectual development. Self-esteem issues can be directly linked to feeling intimidated. Intimidation is a feeling of fear that plays out in the mind of an intimidated person. African-Americans can fight intimidation by educating ourselves about how our African ancestors are responsible for civilizing this world.

Assimilation can also be an issue in raising intellectual standards. When African-Americans aspire to be like European-Americans, we lose. We psychologically and outwardly project a mindset that "white is right." When the values, morals, dogmas, and ideas we see and learn are Caucasian, as African-Americans we devalue our own values, morals, dogma, and ideas.

One outstanding, "in your face" example of this assimilation is the hair-relaxing process used by African-American women and girls. Many African-American women say that they do it because their hair, in its natural state, is difficult to maintain. This attitude affects our intellectual capacity to respect our roots and ancestry. The straighter the hair, the more many African-American women feel that their attractiveness is enhanced. Straight hair is considered "good hair," while more natural, coarse hair—which the majority African-American women have—is considered not to be good hair. Based on this reality, Caucasian people have "good hair." This conclusion means that "good hair" is not naturally attached to the scalps of African-American women and girls. Many of our women must go through a sacrifice or the killing of our natural hair to assimilate to have "good hair," the presumed European-American standard of beauty. The psychological impact of just this hair scenario alone is extremely problematic for intellectual development; we must conclude that many believe that loving and living our African heritage is totally out of the question.

CHAPTER 5:
THE LACK OF KNOWLEDGE, ABOUT OUR HERITAGE

A people without a thorough understanding of its cultural heritage is a lost people. That lack of cultural integrity has been an obvious issue for many African-Americans. The morality of being a respectable people seems to be a major hurdle for African-Americans as well. Cultural integrity is defined by the morals and values that have been culturally established. Africa is a very important continent in the journey to reclaim the morals and values of our people. We are the authors and innovators of civilization for the world.

Many African-Americans are not aware of this fact and are fixated on the European being the author of every facet of life. This creates an intellectual barrier, because one's knowledge base becomes that of an intellectually tardy people. It is not intellectually healthy and is totally unacceptable to have the culture and heritage of African-Americans defined by others that are not of African descent. Much of what is defined in modern-day history books is that Europeans became the mothers and fathers of civilization through the European Renaissance. The European Renaissance came about in the fifteenth century after the so-called "Dark Ages," which was the time of Moorish rule in Europe. The Moors brought civilization, architecture, mathematics, science, and other skills to Europe—and mainly Spain. The Moors were an African and Negroid people. To learn more about the Moors read *The Golden Age of the Moors* by Dr. Ivan Van Sertima.

The first European Renaissance, the age of learning, provided an opportunity for the many gifts of the Moors to be expanded throughout Europe. This renaissance allowed the Europeans to write in the annals of history that they are the authors of all things civil and academic. According to Dr. Walter Williams, author of *The Historical Origins of Christianity,*

Europe was one of the most illiterate places on the planet prior the Renaissance era.

A lack of cultural integrity continues to play a key role in the state of intellect in the African-American community. A lack of respect for academia also remains a thorn in the side of the African-American community. It remains unpopular to be smart, especially among some African-American youth today. This apathy toward academics leads to a lack of scholastic standards established in the household. A lack of respect for academics gives rise to a decline in intellect.

Taking pride in being smart and intellectual is essential to establishing one's knowledge of self. Knowledge of self is a highly important part of life for all people, but it is especially important for African-Americans at this time. When we have a thorough knowledge of self, we become more empowered, more self-assured, and more historically astute. The intellectual impact of having a complete knowledge of self cannot be underestimated.

CHAPTER 6:
THE VISION OF YOURSELF
AND YOUR INTELLECT

The phrase "believe in yourself" is very cliché, but it is extremely apropos to building your intellect. Believing in yourself is a critical aspect of building your intellect, because belief builds confidence. You must be confident in your intellectual abilities to allow it to be visible to others. Allow your belief in yourself to be the motivating factor in your quest to build your intellect.

You should never put a capstone on learning. Before you can believe in yourself or your intellectual growth and abilities, you must love yourself first. An extension of this love for yourself must encompass a love for your people and your heritage. Again, this requires a thorough knowledge of self. The love that I am referring to includes pride, dignity, and intellectual greatness. *Love* can be an over-rated word and can lose its power through misuse. Part of the intellectual problem in the African-American community is that there is a lack of love and respect for one another. We must respect our heritage and people before we can ascertain the belief that our historical heritage is the foundation of intellectual integrity and growth.

Intellectual growth is developed and manifested through the process of building your intellect. I recommend using my intellectual building strategies, which are called the Rice Intellectual Building Blocks. The blocks are Knowledge of Self, Reading, Research, and Vocabulary. Knowledge of Self is having a great knowledge of your cultural and ancestral heritage and history. This knowledge must be visible in your daily life in the form of pride and dignity. Reading is simply being able to read, comprehend, and apply information from a variety of literary sources. Reading is the fundamental cornerstone of intellect. Research is the willingness to go beyond your general knowledge base by conducting studious investigations aimed at new discoveries and interpretation of facts. The final building block is Vocabulary. Build your vocabulary by learning and using new words. The dictionary is the best source of vocabulary building. Once you learn a new word, you must incorporate this word in your active vocabulary.

If you adhere to the Rice Intellectual Building Blocks, I guarantee that your overall level of intellect will increase. These blocks are tools that you can use and share for the betterment of yourself as well others, especially those in your household. You may already utilize some aspect of the Rice Intellectual Building Blocks in your life, but if this is not the case, I strongly suggest that you start today.

CHAPTER 7:
THE ARTHURS AND SOURCES
OF YOUR THOUGHTS

It is very important to be cognizant of the sources of your thoughts. Mainstream media is instrumental in institutionalizing thoughts and perceptions in the public on a daily basis. Oftentimes we allow what we see on television, which may be a form of propaganda, to become the foundation of fact for us.

An example of this would be the depiction of African-Americans in television, film, and hip-hop music videos. In hip-hop videos, young men are depicted as thugs and misogynistic. African-American women are depicted as whore-like and unintelligent. The disturbing aspect of this hip-hop video example is that young people show signs that they believe these images represent them accurately. Young African-American men have begun to embrace and publically display a thug-like persona and embrace a disrespectful, misogynist mindset. Young women begin to think it is okay and normal for them to have and display mindless, whore-like tendencies.

These actions point to a lack of intellect and self-respect because they reflect an adherence to detrimental stereotypical images of African-Americans. There is obviously a lack of objective intellectual understanding. Allowing mainstream media sources to enter into your dendrites without a critical investigation can be intellectually devastating. Dendrites are treelike extensions of neurons located in your brain that receive information. Therefore, you must be the gatekeeper of what outside forces you allow to shape your intellect.

Cultural folklore is another form of communication that we allow to define our thoughts. An excellent example of this would be when a member of your family tells you as a youngster that if you get your head wet out in the rain you would "catch a cold." The reality is that a cold is generated by a germ and not by rainwater. Many of us go into our adult lives believing such cultural folklore to be fact. Folklore does have a place in many cultures today, but to allow folklore to be the foundation of your intellectual reality is counterproductive. However, using cultural folklore as an aspect to define or gain intellectual understanding from an anthropological standpoint can be highly useful. My point is that folklore must be kept in its proper perspective; it cannot be the sum of your intellectual development.

It is my observation that we as African-Americans do not need to continue to allow nonacademic or nonscholastic information to be static pillars in our intellectual growth. Facts are the most profound set of truths that the intellectual mind can absorb. Fact-based information must be the foundation of our intellectual growth and development. Researching the facts has to become the norm when it comes to strengthening your intellect. I learned many years ago that fact-finding research gave me an intellectual edge that is still unmatched to this day.

There are occasions when nonacademic information can provide intellectual growth, such as information we get from observing nature. The only problem with this is that oftentimes we ignore what nature has to teach us and engulf ourselves in a more nonessential, Western style of thought processing. If we really knew the facts about our anthropological history as a Negroid people, it would enhance our intellectual capacity instantly.

CHAPTER 8:
HOW DOES MASS SOCIETY AFFECT YOUR THOUGHTS?

A huge intellectual development barrier for African-Americans is the effects of mass society on our thoughts. I have systematically broken this down into three factors: images, standards, and defining reality. Let's start with images. The depiction of African-Americans in the media is not directly controlled by African-Americans. We can, however, control how we present ourselves to the world on a personal basis outside the media. We allow others to define our image by providing others with stereotypical imagery.

Let's consider the "saggin'" pants that are currently defining many of our youth today. A fad is one thing, but the degradation of a people is a totally different scenario. The "saggin'" pants issue has escalated beyond a fad. It has now become a defining factor of the image of our young men. In today's society, image is everything! African-American women are depicted as loose women and downright unrespectable in various media outlets such as cinema, reality shows, and situation comedies. These images suggest a lack of intelligence. Women with integrity would have a better sense of dignity and not allow women to be portrayed in such a negative way.

We cannot simply write this off as a capitalistic opportunity. At some point intellect must kick in and establish a new precedent for African-American women. African-American men must continue to step up and be real fathers to their sons and to other young men whose fathers are absent. We must instill in our young men that it is cool to be smart and to become an intellectual. The "saggin'" pants epidemic is one of the most degrading fads that I have ever witnessed in my lifetime.

Integrity, respect, dignity, intellect, and cultural pride must be established as the standards for our cultural totems. That our reality is defined by another race of people is shocking as well as alarming. But this is the scenario that is taking place today for African-Americans. When mainstream America defines the reality for African-Americans, it usually means that there are not any redeeming qualities about African-Americans. Our reality becomes fatherless children and fractured households. Our reality becomes that we are not intellectuals, but that we are athletes, rappers, thugs, and gang bangers. Although many aspects of the aforementioned statements have some truth to them, the statements do not define us exclusively as the Western world depicts. We must take control of our identity by building our intellect and redefining it.

CHAPTER 9:
HOW TO DETECT ARROGANT RHETORIC

Having the ability to detect rhetoric is a key part of building your intelligence. Most rhetoric that we hear today in the African-American community can be broken down into buzzwords and catchphrases. An excellent example is the catchphrase "black people are like crabs in a barrel," which sadly defines the mentality of African-Americans toward one another when it comes to success and respect. This particular catchphrase is not only true, but it defines what logical thought is in general for African-Americans. The truthful aspects of this phrase, which tend not to be discussed, are the lasting effects of the brutality of slavery.

The psychological effects of slavery embedded a mentality of self-hatred in African people. We are not a united people and our inability to become a unified people has plagued our community for over a century now in the United States. Authors Omar Reid, Sekou Mims, and Larry Higginbottom define this psychological challenge as "Post Traumatic Slavery Disorder" in their book *Post Traumatic Slavery Disorder: Definition, Diagnosis and Treatment.* The psychological impact of slavery on African-Americans cannot be overlooked and warrants further investigation by all of us.

There are some of us who promote and sincerely applaud the success of others, however this "crabs in a barrel" mentality is very much alive today. Once you are able to understand and acknowledge that slavery has played a major role in how African-American people see one another, you will begin to understand how this catchphrase has credibility today. But the mentality reflected in this catchphrase gives rise to a defeatist attitude about our own race and can also be attributed to the lack of intellectual growth and development.

Insensitivity is another key obstacle to intellectual growth. Many people use insensitive, arrogant behavior and rhetoric to force themselves on others. Every person can learn something from another person, but being insensitive can be problematic in personal and intellectual growth. Insensitivity can cause a proud individual to act as if his or her way of thinking is the only way of thinking, and this behavior can cause long-term issues for African-Americans whose aspirations are to assimilate and become more European-American or Caucasian.

I am not faulting European-Americans for being who they are. I am, however, sending an alert to Africans to be who we are meant to be: sensitive to others and a dignified people. Insensitivity can be attributed to a supremacist mentality and lifestyle. Back in the late 1990s, I was taking courses at Indiana University Purdue University at Indianapolis to finish up my Education degree. I was taking the course "Education in a Pluralistic Society". One day we were having a class discussion on educating African-American and Hispanic children in various major cities across the United States. My professor, who is a European-American woman, continued to label these children as "inner-city" youth.

I took offense to this labeling and made the comment that the term *inner-city* is a racist one used to label my people negatively. My professor said that *inner-city* is not racist label and that I was reaching for something that was not there. She went on to articulate that *inner-city* only refers to the downtown aspect of a city. I then ask her where she lived, and she replied that she lived in downtown Bloomington, Indiana.

As a graduate of Indiana University, which is located in Bloomington, I was very familiar with the downtown area of that city. I then said to her that, based on her definition of *inner-city*, she is an inner-city adult. She looked at me with an ashamed and embarrassed look on her face. She went on to tell me that I am a "master of verbal persuasion" and that she was wrong in using the "inner-city" label in reference to African-Americans. She had openly displayed her insensitivity to how this term affects me and other African-Americans.

She was not comfortable, to say least, when I successfully labeled her as "inner-city."

White supremacy in the United States is still very much alive in U.S. society. The reaction to President Barak Obama being elected as the first African-American president serves as an excellent example. Many European-Americans are in fear that their "white way" of life is slipping away. The demographics of the United States are changing, with people of color becoming the majority population and the European-American population becoming the minority. People of color outnumber Caucasians globally by about fourteen to one, and this ratio is increasing as I write this book.

Many Caucasians in America continue to question President Obama's citizenship, intelligence, decision making, and ability to lead. The fact that President Obama is an African-American automatically gives fuel to the mentality of white supremacy, which remains an unyielding faction in American fiber today.

White privilege plays a major role in the formation of the intellect of African-Americans, because when white privilege is applied, it causes an inferiority complex for African people. We begin to take on the mindset that we cannot achieve because white privilege will block our social, political, economic, and educational advancements. Let's use the sports world as an example. European-American athletes are typically depicted as being intelligent. An adjective such as "cerebral" is a staple when describing many white athletes. On the other hand, African-American athletes are typically described as being "athletic" and not possessing the intellectual capacity of European-American athletes.

To counter white privilege, as African-Americans need to implement superior intellect and build up our knowledge of facts in as many disciplines as possible, especially the disciplines of history, anthropology, and linguistics.

The discipline of history provides factual information about the greatness of our African ancestors the ancient Egyptians and how they are the progenitors of all civilization. This information provides facts to combat the myth of a Eurocentric world. The discipline of anthropology—the study of a people and their culture over time—provides an intellectual foundation of knowledge and an understanding of Caucasians as part of humanity. This information lays a foundation for understanding white privilege as well as white supremacy. The discipline of linguistics— the study of language and human speech—provides intellectual knowledge of the origin of language, which is Egyptian. Once you understand and embrace the greatness of being an African, you become impervious to white privilege and white supremacy. Always remember that the affirmation of authority is to be able to create other people's life experiences and force them to comply according to those created experiences.

CHAPTER 10:
THE DIFFERENCE BETWEEN BELIEFS AND FACTS

Understanding the difference between belief and facts is an essential cornerstone to building your intellect. What is reality? Reality is what is factually true and what is spiritually true. Spiritual truth has absolutely nothing to do with religion. Religion has done a masterful job of dictating what reality is, with or without facts. This is why you must set religion to the side in order to understand and encompass facts, to define your own reality, and ultimately to build your intellect. You must control your reality as much as you consciously can and not allow others to control your reality.

A huge part of being in control of your reality is having an understanding and knowledge of universal and historical truths. Sometimes we get caught up in a belief system that is a barrier to intellectual growth and development. You can believe whatever you desire, but if your beliefs do not line up with historical facts or truths, then you should reexamine the belief system that has affected your intellectual growth thus far. You must be prepared to do research to discover and reaffirm historical facts.

William Bennett, the former Secretary of Education during the Reagan Administration, has been quoted as saying, "To be ignorant of history is to be intellectually defenseless". This is an outstanding and downright truthful quote. Building your intellect is a laborious task, but the reward of having a superb intellect is well worth it. Embracing factual information is one essential cornerstone of intellectual growth and development. Dr. Walter Williams, author of *The Historical Origin of Christianity* and *The Historical Origin of Islam,* write this about facts:

Facts are:

1. Stronger than argument.
2. More profound than reasoning.

3. More dependable than opinion.
4. Silences disputes.
5. Supersedes predictions.
6. Facts always end the argument.

I would like to add another point to this list: "Obliterates beliefs." These seven points are essential building blocks for gaining an intellectual advantage when it comes to understanding and the application of facts. The various courts of law throughout the world consistently focus on what the facts are for each case that comes before them. Again, you can believe whatever your heart desires, but always remain aware that if your beliefs are not factually based, you have nothing but a belief, and that is it.

CHAPTER 11:
WHY IT IS IMPORTANT TO HAVE AN OWNERSHIP MENTALITY

To change or enhance your intellectual prowess, develop an ownership mentality. Having an ownership mentality means that you own your thoughts and that your mental filters are always alert to filter out garbage. The journey to developing this mentality begins with taking control of your mind and your thinking process. As long as someone else controls or dictates your thinking, you are a slave to that person or ideology. Many of us simply give control of our minds and thinking over to others on a daily basis. One of the key factors in preventing this is to question everything. Always remain alert and aware of anything and everything that happens and is said around you. This will help you to hone in on what is beneficial to your intellectual growth and what is detrimental to it. Yes, this means questioning religion, politics, social values, and anything else in your life that can have an effect on your thinking.

Have you ever thought about how, in all lecture-type forums, the audience is provided with a question–and-answer segment as part of the presentation—except in a church setting? Why is it that the practice and application of medicine is based on the Caucasian male? Why is it that the prison population in the United States of America is overwhelmingly African-American male? These are just a few questions that point out areas of using mental control and intellectual growth.

Never ask a question without having an intellectual game plan behind it to promote your personal intellectual growth. Questioning various aspects of life is always a good thing for intellectual development and for building an ownership mentality. An ownership mentality is also a tremendous asset to have when it comes to having great self-esteem. Moreover your self-esteem can be affected by the level of your intelligence;

the more knowledge you have, the more your self-confidence will soar. The closer that you become to achieving an ownership mentality, the more control you have of your thoughts and your overall intellectual capacity.

It also is a good practice to expand your general knowledge base socially, politically, and historically. Never place a cap on your intellectual growth. I never classify myself as an expert on any subject or discipline. I will be the first to tell you that I am a sponge; I love to soak up intellectually stimulating information. The road to obtaining ownership mentality is a challenging one, but the reward will transform your life forever.

CHAPTER 12:
THE DIFFERENCE BETWEEN LOGIC AND COMMON SENSE

A fact-based intellectual foundation gives you a mental edge that is life changing. Building your intellectual foundation on facts is extremely profound because facts are just that: the facts. You can choose to believe whatever you desire, but facts make your beliefs dissipate. Building your intellect on untruths or nonfactual information is extremely dangerous to your intellectual growth. When logic or intellect is based on faith, you are setting yourself up to be mentally manipulated. Walking—or making mental conclusions—by faith and not fact is also detrimental. Oftentimes we believe in things that we have not researched to find the truth or facts for ourselves. This is why I encourage you not to follow anyone except yourself.

Stop falling prey to naivety and become intellectually stronger.

Faith-based knowledge does not provide the intellectual enhancement or cultivation that I feel is necessary to becoming a true intellectual. Intellect seems to put fear in some of us because we continue to run away from it. You can believe that I am physically writing this book using a bar of soap, but the fact is that I am using a pen. It does not matter what you believe; what matters is what the facts are and whether those facts can be substantiated with research and bibliography. If you continue to base your intellect on faith as oppose to facts that is definitely your prerogative.

Increasing your intellect also requires you to move beyond common sense. Common sense is simply the knowledge and application of life experiences that are common to all people. Striving to go beyond being common should be the goal of any person who desires to raise his or her intellect. As a society, we collectively conclude that everyone understands and applies common sense to their daily living. We in the African-American community can no longer settle on living day to day on just common sense. We must live intellectually at the highest level that we can ascertain from our ancestors, the ancient Egyptians.

Because the ancient Egyptians were a Negroid people, their blood runs in us and Africans all over the world today. Modern-day Egyptians do not represent the ancient Negroid Egyptian stock. Let us move on now that we have established our ancestral link. The ancient Egyptians were the most advanced people to ever walk the face of the Earth during the time of antiquity. I am not going to go into a history lesson in this book, but I encourage you to research, learn, and embrace our African ancestors, the ancient Egyptians. The more you know and internalize, the more you will reach new heights in intellectual sharpness and in your understanding of your cultural heritage.

CHAPTER 13:
HOW TO CATEGORIZE YOUR THOUGHTS

Categorizing your thoughts is a rewarding practice that has increased my intellectual fortitude. Some may ask how you categorize your thoughts. I have found over the past twenty-plus years of intellectual training and development that there are three main categories of thought: academic, cultural, and general. Categorizing your thoughts in the academic category helps to build scholastic aptitude. When thoughts of an academic nature come across your mind, organize them accordingly. Academic thoughts build intellect because they are based on scholarship and help increase learning and knowledge.

You cannot be afraid to be smart. You have to have a desire to be smart, which involves allowing academic thoughts to help educate you. Learn as much as you can from these thoughts, and always yearn for more. To help cultivate an academic thought process, you must continue to research and read about topics that promote intellectual stimulation. Select books that challenge your mind as well as the way you formulate your thoughts. Research information that will help you substantiate knowledge that you have gained or that you are seeking. Reading is truly fundamental, but research is the backbone of knowledge, wisdom, and understanding.

We also categorize our thoughts based on culture. The word *culture* can be defined and applied in variety of ways. I am going to narrow its application to race, specifically. Different races view the world from different perspectives. These different perspectives give life to a multitude of ways of thinking. In the African-American community, it is not uncommon to hear conversations about owning our own business and no longer working for someone else. We often converse with one another about building our own financial empire. However, our cultural thought process tells us that we are consumers and that we will always be consumers, not owners. We dream big as a culture and as a people, but our cultural thought process keeps us handcuffed—primarily mentally handcuffed.

A couple of issues affect our cultural thoughts: institutionalized white supremacy and a lack of equal employment opportunities. If you do not understand white supremacy, then you are at tremendous psychological disadvantage. I highly recommend that you read Dr. Francis Cress Welsing's book *The Isis Papers* to gain a greater understanding of white supremacy and its effect on people of color.

An example of institutional white supremacy is the slogan many European-Americans have used since the election of Barak Obama: "We want our country back." This statement is very clear. The "our" in this statement excludes African-Americans or all other people of color. The European-Americans who say this slogan do not want a United States of America with an African-American as its leader. Statements like this will continue to be justified as not agreeing with the politics of

President Barak Obama, but the disciplines of history and anthropology reveal the truth and the roots of statements such as this. The endorsers of this type of statement bask in the glow of European-Americans leading everything in this country, and they want to keep it that way.

Socioeconomic barriers can play a major role in the cultural categorization of our thoughts. Many of us are not in a socioeconomic condition to achieve greater wealth or improve our socioeconomic status. This has a tremendous effect on our cultural categorization of our thoughts. We must change the way we think in order to change the negative aspects of our African-American community.

Finally, we come to the general categorization of your thoughts. The general categorization of thought includes everything else outside of academic and cultural categorizations. I recommend having a healthy balance of all three, with the exception of academic categorization having a slight edge. Your cultural way of thinking should be laced with a thorough knowledge of self, as I have explained previously in this book. I encourage you to always strive for intellectual greatness and never cave in to the psychological barriers of American society. As Africans living in America, we come from a proud and illustrious people. I challenge you to continue to find out why.

CHAPTER 14:
ELEVATE YOUR PERSONAL CONVERSATIONS

Each day most of us have many conversations with our family and friends. If you take the time to assess conversations, you will find out that there really is not much depth to them. There are three main topics in adult male conversation: women, sports, and money. I started doing a case study with this in mind in the late 1990s, and I still do it today. What I do is enter a conversation with a group of African-American men; the discussion usually centers around one of those three topics. I then attempt to elevate the discussion with topics such as white supremacy, African history, teaching Black history to our children, or coming together to build a business coalition. The moment I begin to do this, I start to notice others becoming uncomfortable with the conversation. It seems as if there is not any substance in the conversation that promotes intellectual stimulation.

I am using men in this example, but the same holds true for our women as well. We need to actively engage ourselves in conversations with more substance and expand the focal point of our discussions in general. Many of our conversations remain mundane. I am a co-owner of an educational consulting firm in Charlotte, North Carolina. Over the years of providing workshops and seminars on various topics, I have noticed that oftentimes I have to use the Rice Knowledge Tree to help participants gain a greater understanding of various topics. The Rice Knowledge Tree is concept I created to illustrate how to graduate from a mundane way of thinking and from a mundane conversation. The branches of the tree represent what I call Branch-Knowledge. This means that your knowledge is limited because you have not gotten to the "root." Root-Knowledge, on the other hand, is a term I use to define a 360-egree understanding of a topic.

Allow me to apply the topic of the image of African-American women in today's hip-hop culture to the Rice Knowledge Tree. People with Branch-Knowledge conclude that the rappers are disrespectful and portray African-American woman as pieces of meat in their music videos as well as their lyrics. Although this may be true, Root-Knowledge informs us that African-Americans do not control the industry of hip-hop, especially the distribution of the genre. Therefore we now can conclude that non-African-Americans dictate what hip-hop is played on the radio and what the image of African-American women will be in hip-hop music videos. (I realize that I have referenced hip-hop a number of times in this book, but the current state of hip-hop really does not sit well with me. For the record, I love the genre of hip-hop, especially "old-school" hip-hop that is intellectually based.)

We must challenge one another to raise our conversations by incorporating a higher order of thinking. This thinking comes from building up your intellect. I am not suggesting discontinuing talking about topics of humor and fun; however, I am suggesting that an expansion of the use of more substantive topics is in order. Presenting intellectual challenges within your conversation is always a positive for intellectual growth.

CHAPTER 15:
HOW TO MANAGE YOUR MENTAL DATA

Learning how to manage your mental data is an essential pillar in intellectual development. As we navigate this journey called life, we continue to absorb a huge amount of mental data. Some of the data we absorb is beneficial, but a great deal of it is not. We must learn to delete mental files of data that do not promote intellectual growth.

Oftentimes we hold on to things in our mind that prevent us from achieving our goals. We tend to hold on to information that keeps us in a "slave" state of mind, which means that you think mainstream society has your best interests at heart. You must do an internal evaluation of your mind periodically to make the necessary deletions. Negative or unbeneficial mental data can affect your self-esteem, the way you perceive others, and your perception of your own people.

Making a personal evaluation of your mentality is also an important part of your journey to intellectual supremacy. I have personally trained my mind to expunge intellectual blockers and keep the information that provides intellectual stamina. A great example of intellectual blockers is to believe that human civilization started in Europe and that the history of Africa is insignificant. You must apply the Rice Intellectual Building Blocks, defined previously in this book, if you want to see a change in your intellect. Cultivating your intellectual growth requires you to expand your understanding and maximize your "overstanding" of the world around you.

Mathematics and science should join the disciplines previously mentioned—history, anthropology, and linguistics—as the top disciplines to aid you in this cultivation process. I am not suggesting that you enroll in classes at your local community college or university; I am suggesting that you utilize your local library.

As a father of two wonderful children, I do activities that cultivate their minds daily. It is my obligation as a parent to build the intellects of my children as well. Seek the literary resources that provide a challenge to your intellect. Becoming smarter, wiser, and mentally sharp are worthy intellectual goals. The cultivation of your intellectual growth will lead to a new level of discovery. New discoveries should become commonplace. We navigate through this life thinking we are knowledgeable of certain things, but when we experience a new intellectual discovery, our understanding changes immediately.

I wrote this book to educate you the reader on how to avoid Intellectual Sterilization. I also wrote it to help my people become a smarter race from an intellectual perspective. I trust that this book will serve as your guide to discover the birth to your hierarchy of intellectualism.

Ma'at Hotep.

BIBLIOGRAPHY

Browder, Anthony. *Nile Valley Contribution to Civilization.* Washington D.C.: The Institute of Karmic Guidance, 1992.

Finegan, Edward. *Language: Its Structure and Use.* Belmont, CA: Wadsworth Publishing, 2003.

Hacker, Andrew. *Two Nations Black and White Separate, Hostile, Unequal.* New York: Ballantine Books, 1995.

Hassan-El, Kashif Malik. *The Willie Lynch Letter and the Making of a Slave.* Chicago: Frontline Distribution International, 1999.

Herrnstein, Richard, and Charles Murray. *The Bell Curve.* New York: The Free Press, 1994.

Kunjufu, Jawanza. *Countering the Conspiracy to Destroy Black Boys.* Volume 4. Chicago: African American Images, 1995.

Latif, Sultan, and Naimah Latif. *Slavery: The African American Psychic Trauma.* Chicago: Latif Communications Group, 1994.

Reid, Omar, Sekou Mims, and Larry Higginbottom. *Post Traumatic Slavery Disorder.* Charlotte, N.C.: Conquering Books, 2005.

Van Sertima, Ivan. *They Came Before Columbus.* New York: Random House, 1976.

Welsing, Francis Cress. *The Isis Papers.* Chicago: Third World Press, 1992.

Williams, Walter. *The Historical Origin of Christianity.* Chicago: Maathian Press, 1998.

Woodson, Carter. *The Mis-Education of the Negro.* Washington D.C.: Africa World Press, 1990.

www.ingramcontent.com/pod-product-compliance
Lightning Source LLC
Chambersburg PA
CBHW021239280526
45784CB00005B/2154